SOUL POETRY

BY KATHERINE BROWN

SOUL POETRY

This book is dedicated to anyone who ever felt like they weren't good enough, even when they gave their all to another soul.

I used to get asked by someone very special if I had written anything lately. This is dedicated to them as well.

Life is too short to settle.

So be your biggest fan, even if you hate yourself.

Poetry, for some, means certain things, and for others, it is an escape.

Anyone can write down what they are thinking, making it a type of poetry.

Life is what you make it, and poetry is my life and my escape.

Please enjoy the shortness of some of my life pleasures, or in some cases, my fears.

Table of Contents

HOLIDAY

What was the best thing about Christmas? The present, kids would say

The lights on the tree, others would say.

Putting the cookies out or staying up to see Santa.

You ask me, it was the poems my dad wrote us every year.

They were always the thing I looked forward to the most.

Not everyone has family.

Not everyone has a Christmas.

My Christmas was the love of a man who would give his family a gift they could remember forever...

Poetry

RUNNING

Soles of my shoes beat beat beating on the ground.

Moving forward through the world.

The pavement is hitting just right under our soles.

Our shoes are beating the ground.

Our feet are absorbing the blows.

Legs carrying us forward.

The freedom of running with nothing but peace around.

Wind is whipping past, singing us its song.

Soles of my shoes beat beat beating on the ground.

Feeling nothing but peace while running over the world.

TRUTH

For the truth of it all was written in the stars, burning oh so bright that night.

The flames in the pit let everyone know,

The truth of life, not of love itself.

The truth of love is that it hurts.

Love burns so very bright

The never-ending glow until it dies.

The flame of the fire never lasts forever, always needing to be stoked.

The brightness of the stars is all but a lie, thinking they are alive when in fact they are only burning so bright because they are dead.

Truth in the matter is, it is all the pain of the world when you're on fire, dying.

Lies and greed are the same as truth and love.

Some only give the truth so that they can be seen burning a little brighter.

BRIGHT

The world is so bright when I see your smile.

My world is so bright when I make you smile.

Your laugh makes me smile.

Your laugh brings me happiness.

Brightness is a good morning message.
Brightness is a good night message.

My happiness is you.

My happiness was always with you.

Butterflies in my stomach when we would kiss.

My life is burning so bright with you in it.
Brightness is all of you with all of me.

The flame is no longer bright.

The flame had dimmed and gone out.

Brightness lasts only as long as you stoke the flame that burns inside you.

FRESH

First breath of fresh air in over a month.

No longer shaking as I inhale.

Heart rate not elevated, beating normally.

My heart is not breaking with every thought that crosses my mind.

Hope is slowly rising back into my life.

Slowly feeling the peace from within again.
Hoping that the fresh breaths continue,

Wanting nothing more than you.

To feel so relaxed with fresh air moving through my lungs.

No Panic, only Peace.

No Pain, only the fresh air that is left.

NIGHTS

My nights aren't what they once were.

They are shorter now, yet oh so much longer all the same.

My nights are so cold and dark.

My nights are full of screams and terror.

Full of the tears that stream down my face from worry.

Loneness is creeping in to steal the last of the warmth.

A test every night to see if I can survive,

Nights swallowing me whole.

The waves of darkness are trying to drown me.

My nights never seem to end.

Nights now bleed into days, swallowing me whole.

KATHERINE BROWN

DAYS AND NIGHTS

The days seem longer without you.

The nights are endless when you are away.

Tears flow freely nonetheless.

Music playing all lyrics, reminding me,

The glass is without you.

Praying you will come home,

Crying, knowing you won't.

Noises echo off the empty walls.

Pictures that were taken are removed.

Life feels empty without.

I know I'll survive.

Doesn't mean I want to.

Days dragging by.

Nights are freezing, and an endless void.

My heart is broken,

Day and Night.

TEARS

Tears falling down my face.

Rolling down my cheeks, staining my shirt.

My heart is heavy with unexplained pain.

Screams ripping from my throat,

My whole body is shaking,

Falling apart at the seams,

Craving a hug to keep me together.

The walls are the only thing that hears what is happening.

Pillow case soaked through,

Wishing for a simple, unshaking breath of air.

My chest wants to explode.

My heart is beating harder and harder.

My world is crumbling down around me.

Tears streaming down my face.

My world is water from all the tears that have made me fall apart.

PEACE

All I want is a little bit of peace.

Peace in the rain while holding your hand,

Peace in bed while being held.

Peace isn't always easy.

Peace comes when you least expect it,

But also disappears just as quickly.

Little things sometimes bring you the most peace,

Dancing in the rain, bringing peace to the soul, washing away the bad.

Riding in the same vehicle as the one you love is a simple peace.

Standing in a river, the water rushing around you.

You were my peace.

My peace has left.

Now it's time to find my own peace again.

LIGHT

The light shone a little brighter today.

The warmth from it was kind.

The light scares away the darkness.

Light scares away the shadows that try to swallow you.

Heaven shines with the brightest light.

The light from heaven makes us feel safe.

Stars lighting the sky, giving us wonder.

Adventure awaits to be guided by light.

Smiles lightening people's day.

Brightness in some eyes brings us hope.

Light can be everywhere you look.

The light shines brightest when you are near.

You were the light that guided me; now my light is dim.

NOISE

When a tree falls in the forest, if no one is around, does it make a sound?

When you cry alone in the dark, if no one is around, do you make a sound?

When you scream into a storm, does the thunder cover the noise?

When your heart breaks, does the person who did the breaking hear it?

Noise is everywhere.

All sound is noise.

Does noise ever bring you peace?

Or does noise just bring destruction? Noise brings me anxiety.

Noise brings me guilt.

Silence is what we crave,

The peace from noise.

DARK

I was never afraid of the dark,

Until the day you left.

I was never scared of the dark,

Until the day you said goodbye.

I was never scared of the dark,

Until my entire world collapsed.

The dark terrifies me now.

Every noise is making me want to scream.

I was never scared of the dark,

Until I went to sleep that night.

The darkness swallowed me whole, eating all the warmth.

The shadows tried to kill me, laughing at the screams.

I was never afraid of the dark,

Until all that was left was darkness with no light.

WORLD

The world is different today.

Seems sad and scared.

Nothing feels the same.

Yet does all at the same time.

My world is spinning with no end in sight. Promises in mind but never given.

Words spoken but never delivered.

The world is different,

Empty, feeling, and cold.

Words spoken but never received. Loneliness is swallowing me up, falling, Spinning out of control,

Drowning in the darkness,

Seeking out the light,

Nothing shining through,

Voices in the distance.

Darkness in the world is swallowing me whole.

Darkness in the world is eating me alive.

The world is killing me, the world is different,
but the same.

DROWNING

Trying to keep my head above the waves that are crashing down.

Counting the time between to come up for air.

Darkness is grabbing me, pulling me under.

Screams ripping from my throat,

Salt covering my face from tears of losing the battle to the darkness.

Breaths coming faster and faster, Gasping, trying to breathe.

Drowning in this thing called life.

Drowning in the darkness, looking for the light,

Knowing the light has left,

Knowing drowning is all that is left.

SOUL

Our souls are a fickle thing.

Our minds are fighting it all.

The pull to another.

The collapse of our false selves, looking, exploring,

Feeling the world out.

Never knowing, never understanding,

Until the other half is found.

Until we feel complete again.

Our souls perfect match, fitting together like two puzzle pieces,

Soul-bound adventures.

MUSIC

The vibration moving through our bodies,

The flow and beat,

Swaying to it all.

Music is life itself.

The feeling of peace or anger.

Music moves the soul.

Artist speaking to you from great depths,

Never know what you feel until you hit play.

SMILE

Not even a small smile on your so tired-looking face.

A small smile that brings such joy to my soul, such a simple joy.

A tiny glint of happiness is rarely shown.

A small smile, nothing more, nothing less. Something so deep.

Just a simple turn of lips that gives simplicity to joy.

Sparking a warmth in my soul,

Just a small smile.

EXHAUSTED

Stumbling through life exhausted,

Feet feel like a burden to pick up,

Legs are heavy and sore.

Exhaustion is a burden to all.

Exhaustion, the death of some.

Not understanding the feeling,

Wanting nothing more than to give in to exhaustion.

Not letting the darkness take control,

Not letting the exhaustion win.

My mind is swimming with the effects of it all.

Exhaustion is swallowing me whole

DEPRESSION

Fighting an internal battle

Fighting the screams that wanted to slip from my lips

Tears slipping free from the corner of my eyes

Fighting a battle that is only visible in the darkness of night

The feeling of exhaustion slips into the simplicity of daily tasks

Wanting nothing more than for the pain inside to stop

Looking for a release

Pain radiating from the body Depression slipping out

Tears streaming down my face

LOVE

A language that all speak.

A soul-craving aspect deep within.

The warmth of love,

Giving butterflies at first sight,

Radiating off you.

A craving you never knew you'd want,

A touch of safety and solidarity,

Love of chaos,

Love of peace,

Love is all that we want it to be.

Sometimes love hurts,

Sometimes it's a peaceful feeling.

Fight for the love you deserve.

RINGS

Rings a metal of such preciousness,

Meaning of survival for some.

Meaning of love for others.

Meanings of the beauty or wealth.

Ring simplicity is in the eye of the wearer.

Something so simple could mean the world.

Each finger represents certain things,

A rock or a simple pattern.

Given the simplicity of such a meaning, only the wearer knows.

Swirls and knots,

Big shiny stones.

The ring says all without saying much at all.

QUIET

The peace of the world is not well-known. Quietness is a bliss that not all get to enjoy,

But you can hear it all around you.

The quietness of the wind when it blows around you.

The quietness of the blades of grass rubbing together, whistling their own song.

The mornings right before the world wakes.

The quietness of sitting alone in the dark,

The quietness of listening to your children breathe while they sleep, dreaming of all kinds of things.

Quiet is the peace of all things around you.

You just have to find it.

YOU

Who are you?

Not as you are a teacher.

Who are you?

I am a country, I am an adventure,

Figuring out who you are is the peace you deserve.

No one can tell you who you are.

People are put into our lives to guide us.

Some get to stay for a long time to help us.

Some are short-term to help us realize who we aren't.

You are you, and not everyone is meant to know the real you.

Just be you, never settle for less than YOU.

POETRY

For the flowers blowing in the wind,

Joy of breathing.

Not always making sense, but feeling oh so right.

Poetry isn't always rhyming.

Sometimes it's the feeling of your being that is really going on inside.

Poetry of peace.

Poetry of depression gives an outlet.

Writing is the outlet that guides you to a peaceful soul.

Literary work in which special intensity

Is given to those who want the intensity of life, the simple way.

Without the hurt, without the sorrow. Poetry at the finest point of simplicity

ENDING

If the world were to end tonight, would you call?

If the world were to end tonight, would you wanna spend your last moments with me?

If the world were to end tonight, would you care if I were alone?

My world ended when you said goodbye.

I crumpled to the ground,

Screaming and crying,

Darkness seeping into my lungs.

My world ended with a simple conversation.

A simple word was said, and my world crashed down.

My body was going through the motions of living while my brain was shut down.

Darkness behind my eyes while everyone continued on.

If the world were to end tonight, would you come home?

FRIENDSHIP

Friendship is the kind of love everyone needs.

Building friendships that can last a lifetime.

People who become family.

The ones who listen to everything you have to say.

The ones who know when something is wrong just by the way you talk,

Just by the way your face looks,

Never being able to hide what you truly feel from those who truly love you.

Friendships that turn to family are the best friendships there are.

DOGS

The only constant thing we have,

They are there every second you need a feeling of peace,

The feeling of a pure connection.

The ones who hear your true feelings,

The crying, the screaming.

The ones that are there during the bad dreams,

A best friend you have from day one.

The adventure partner everyone needs,

The main reason for getting out of bed on certain days.

The reason you feel the sun on your face.

The reason you laugh even when you didn't think it was possible.

Dogs are the true friends of a lifetime.

NIGHT SKY

The night sky is a never-ending abyss of beauty.

A guide that is so easy to follow yet so difficult.

A true peaceful bliss, and all you have to do is look up.

Every star that shines so bright tells a story all of its own.

The moon is so beautiful and bright.

The only thing that is the same no matter where you are in the world.

Never knowing who may be looking up at the same time,

Finding the utmost peace in such a simple thing,

Yet so extravagant.

The night sky is a beautiful wonder for all eyes.

MENTAL HEALTH

The puzzle of confusion,

A trap everyone is looking to escape,

A maze that never seems to end,

A brick wall you want to break down.

Needing help, but no way of being able to ask for it,

Hoping no one sees the struggle you're fighting on the inside.

Feel a scream that wants to tear from your throat,

Tears that burn your eyes, but you won't let them escape,

Drowning in an ocean, the water is swallowing you up.

Darkness is engulfing you, never letting you escape.

Demons whispering nothing but lies to you, making you feel like you're losing the battle.

Mental health awareness needs to be known.

988 suicide and crisis lifeline, don't wait until it's too late.

HOME

A safe place,

Until the darkness tries to swallow you up,

A safe place until the walls feel like they are closing in.

Home is a place for family.

Home is a place for friends.

A safe place,

Your favorite blanket to wrap up in.

Your favorite oversized hoodie.

Home is your true escape from life,

Until life tries to scream in your ear.

Home is what you make it.

Give it your all so you can scream.

This is my home.

MEMORIES

They are such an important thing.

If I had to pick a favorite memory, the task would be too challenging.

Memories sneak up on you when you least expect them.

Some memories slip down your cheeks.

Some make you laugh when you least expect.

I never want to lose my memories.

My memories are my most cherished thing.

Wishing I could watch them like a movie sometimes,

Instead of staring at pictures or old messages.

Memories are all we have of a life we have lived.

Memories are oh so cruel.

CRAVING

A life shared with someone would have been great.

A life shared with someone your soul craved would have been so amazing.

The life you dream of every day.

Never quite getting to grasp it in your hands.

When you do, it is such an amazing feeling of hope,

Of love.

Sharing everything you have with another soul,

The peace of it being in a simple bliss of love.

EYES

Eyes are the way to the soul.

Blue eyes, when you look into them, make you feel like you're swimming in the ocean.

Green eyes make you feel like you are walking in a field of the greenest grass.

Hazel eyes, forever changing depending on the light, taking you for a ride through the mountainside.

Brown eyes, if you stare too long, make you feel like the darkness of them will swallow you whole.

Eyes are the way to a person's soul.

What does your soul say through your eyes?

HEART

The thing that keeps us alive.

We only have one.

We put our hearts through so much.

We give them to other people with the hope that they keep them safe for us.

Hoping they stay in one piece.

Hearts, when they break, make us scream and cry as they explode into a million pieces.

The heart tells the brain what to think,

Giving into its deepest desires.

GIVING UP

Have you ever felt like you weren't going to make it another day?

Have you ever wondered how you were going to get out of bed?

Feeling like you're failing in all things.

Please don't think you're alone.

Get up, get dressed, smile, and laugh.

Show the demons that you are stronger than your worst days.

Pull on the adult pants and put on your war face, never give up, and just keep pushing.

A wise man says that to me a lot.

SLIPPING

Tears are stinging the corners of my eyes,

Sitting down with only my thoughts.

Darkness seeping in at the edge,

Trying to fight the cry that my lips are forming.

My body is shaking like I'm cold, even though I'm not.

The trembling running down my arms to my hands, shaking ever so slightly, making little waves in my coffee cup.

Why when is it when you are alone, do the demons want to come play,

Making you think about all the worst possible things.

Tears are rolling down my cheeks as the darkness takes a drink.

STORM

That fresh scent in the air of a new beginning, becoming oh so promising.

Dark Clouds are slowly snuffing out the sun.

Darkness of night stealing from the day before its time.

Raindrops pinging off the roof, bringing life to the earth.

If you listen closely, you can hear the thunder singing off in the distance.

Darkness is swallowing the light until lightning flashes across the sky,

Making it as bright as day.

The thunder rumbling closer as time continues on,

The storm of a new beginning is raging on in life.

STRANGERS

Someone you don't pay attention to,

Passing by on the sidewalk.

Some smile, some nod their head.

Some acknowledge the existence of others,
while some keep on moving.

Some become friends.

Some just stay strangers.

Strangers are all over until you talk to them.

Then friendships can be made.

Strangers make up the world,

Until kindness is given.

HORSES

You are riding on the trail.

Everything is a blur around you,

Moving so smoothly,

Moving as one.

Two separate entities, two separate minds,

Working as one.

The wind, moving past you, stinging your skin.

Making you feel like you are flying when still on the ground.

Horses, a true escape into the wilds of the unknown,

Taking the trail less traveled on moving as one soul.

ADVENTURE

The adventure of a lifetime could be right around the corner.

You never know until you take the step.

You can't be afraid of something you've never experienced,

Not all adventures start the same.

I can also say not all adventures end the same, either.

Some adventures can last you a lifetime

Some adventures end just as quickly as they begin.

Adventures can be as simple as a road trip.

Simple as a fly through the sky to a new land.

Adventures could be a new love or the start of a family.

Adventures are around every corner, you just have to take the first step.

SNOW

A beautiful thing.

Big white fluffy flakes falling from the sky,
Coating everything in white,

Giving the sense of peace.

The air so still, making whisper quiet outside.

A protective blanket for the earth.

Snow helping bring new life to the world.

At a certain time of the year, can snow be found

Giving a joy to be in nature.

WRITING

For if the depth of one's life can't be listed on. Some pages would make healing so much easier.

If writing everything one was feeling down with a pen on some paper, I would be perfect.

But at last, this is not the case.

The sun shines a little brighter every day,

While the darkness stays at bay, always sitting at the very edge.

Writing is a peaceful way out.

My way of escaping a life I'm not sure I want to live every day

Every day is a struggle that I will fight till the end of time.

Demons and angels waging a war inside me,

Wanting to know who will win.

Writing is my true escape into a world where only peace exists.

PANIC

Over and over again,

Every breath, pulled in shakily,

Wondering when the world will swallow me whole.

Panicking over and over again,

Wanting nothing more than for the panic to stop.

Waves crashing on repeat in my head,

You're not good enough, being shouted all the time.

Panicking over and over again.

All I want is to feel just right.

Hovering over my own body, wondering what did I do wrong.

Panic, all I want to do is hide.

Panic accepting the darkness.

CHAPTERS

Turning the page into a new chapter of life.

Looking back at the old ones, wanting to hang on to them.

Knowing it isn't good for your soul.

New chapters need to start to help us grow.

You will forever have your old chapters.

A grabbing hand that holds onto you,

Taking the next step forward is the only way.

Forever knowing that all you have to do is open the book to look back.

Chapters of your life,

The life we live.

DRINKING

A nice glass of whatever calms you down.

A bottle of beer,

Or a glass of whiskey,

That shot of tequila, Drinking,

Listening to that favorite song on repeat,

Sitting in the garage.

Maybe by a fire surrounded by friends,

Drinking,

A nice glass of whatever calms you down.

A couple of fingers of bourbon,

Nice tall stemmed glass of wine,

Drinking whatever calms you down.

When I'm drinking I'm drinking!

WHISPERING

The wind whispering past the windows.
Demons, whispering in your ear.

People whispering about you.

The darkness whispering what it would like you
to do.

Angels whispering all around you,

Not letting the whispering bother you.

Whispering through life,

Not making a big imprint.

Whispering across the ground as you walk,

Whispering the peace into existence.

SOLO

Enjoy the things of life even if you do them solo.

Start that next adventure, even if you are solo.

Take that vacation even if you have to do it solo.

Being solo doesn't make you weak.

Being solo can make you the strongest person.

Chase your dreams solo,

Hike the trail solo.

Being solo isn't the worst thing in the world.

The peace of the things I have written has put the darkness at bay. Thank you for reading. I hope this has helped you, too.

Rise to the challenge of daily life and just keep pushing through the roadblocks.

Never settle and never doubt yourself.